SQUASH / CALABAZAS

Inés Vaughn
Traducción al español: Ma. Pilar Sanz

PowerKiDS press & **Editorial Buenas Letras**™
New York

Published in 2009 by The Rosen Publishing Group, Inc.
29 East 21st Street, New York, NY 10010

First Edition

Editor: Amelie von Zumbusch
Book Design: Kate Laczynski
Photo Researcher: Jessica Gerweck

Photo Credits: Cover, pp. 1, 12 Shutterstock.com; cover texture, p. 1 © www.istockphoto.com/ Gerry Tarney; pp. 4, 15 © Sean Sprague/Peter Arnold, Inc.; p. 7 © Philip Dowell/Getty Images; p. 8 © www.istockphoto.com/Vera Bogaerts; p. 11 © Michel Zabé/Art Resource, NY; p. 16 © Quentin Bacon/Getty Images; p. 19 © Macduff Everton/Getty Images; p. 20 © Topic Photo Agency IN/Age Fotostock.

Library of Congress Cataloging-in-Publication Data

Vaughn, Inés.
  Squash = Calabazas / Inés Vaughn ; traducción al español, Ma. Pilar Sanz. — 1st ed.
    p. cm. — (Native foods of Latin America)
  Includes index.
  ISBN 978-1-4358-2727-1 (library binding)
  1. Squashes—Juvenile literature. I. Sanz, Ma. Pilar (María Pilar) II. Title. III. Title: Calabazas.
  SB347.V38 2009
  641.3'562098—dc22
                                    2008028399

Manufactured in the United States of America

CONTENTS

CONTENIDO

Squash is a wonderful crop that comes from North America and South America. There are many, many kinds of squash. People eat many parts of the squash plant, too. The fruit, the seeds, and the flowers all taste great. Some dishes are even served in a squash!

La calabaza es un maravilloso cultivo que viene del continente americano. Existen muchas clases de calabazas y la gente come muchas partes distintas de ellas. La pulpa, las semillas, y hasta las flores de las calabazas son muy ricas. ¡Algunos platillos incluso se sirven dentro de las calabazas!

Many kinds of squash are eaten in Latin America. Pear-shaped *ayotes*, with dark green skin and yellow spots, are eaten in Mexico. **Lobed** *güicoys* are found in Mexico and Guatemala. West Indian pumpkins, also called *ahuyamas*, *zapallos*, or *calabazas*, are eaten throughout Latin America.

En Latinoamérica se comen muchas clases de calabazas. En México se comen los ayotes, que tienen forma de pera y una cáscara verde oscuro con manchas amarillas. Las guicoyas con **lóbulos** se encuentran en México y Guatemala. Las calabazas del Caribe, como las ahumayas y los zapallos, se comen en toda Latinoamérica.

All squash grow on **vines**. Squash plants bear yellow or orange flowers. The plants have both male and female flowers. After bees **pollinate** these flowers, fruits begin to form. We often think of squash as a vegetable, but, since it has seeds, **scientists** say it is really a fruit!

Las calabazas son plantas **trepadoras**. Las plantas de las calabazas producen flores amarillas y anaranjadas. Las plantas tienen flores masculinas y femeninas. Las calabazas crecen cuando las abejas **polinizan** estas flores. Normalmente pensamos que las calabazas son una verdura, pero los **científicos** han descubierto que son frutas. Esto es porque las calabazas tienen semillas.

9

Scientists think different groups of Native Americans discovered and began planting different kinds of squash. Squash seeds that are 10,000 years old have been found in Peru, Mexico, and Ecuador. Native Americans valued squash so highly that they made squash-shaped pieces of stone and pottery.

Los científicos dicen que las calabazas fueron cultivadas por muchos grupos indígenas de Latinoamérica. Semillas de calabazas de más de 10,000 años se han encontrado en Perú, México y Ecuador. Las calabazas eran tan valiosas para los indígenas que estos hacían figuras de cerámica y piedra de ellas.

11

Squash seeds were an important food for the Native Americans, too. The Aztecs of Mexico ate many dishes that were made with squash seeds. Today, squash seeds are still found in Mexican dishes, such as *pollo en pipián*. Pumpkin seeds, or *pepitas*, are also a common snack.

Las semillas de calabaza eran un alimento muy importante para los indígenas. Los aztecas, en México, comían muchos platillos hechos con semillas de calabaza. Hoy, muchos platos mexicanos, como el pollo al pipián, siguen usando las semillas. Además, las pepitas, o semillas de calabaza tostadas, son un bocadillo muy popular.

There are many Latin American squash dishes. Green squash called *chayotes* are often cooked and made into salads. You can also make a great soup from chayotes. West Indian pumpkins taste great fried or **mashed**. They are also used to make sweet dishes, like flan.

En Latinoamérica, hay muchos platillos con calabaza. Los chayotes, calabazas de color verde claro, se usan en ensaladas y sopas. Las calabazas del Caribe son muy sabrosas cuando están fritas o en **puré**. También se usan para hacer algunos postres, como el flan.

15

16

Squash are often cut up and cooked with cream and chiles in Mexico. In Argentina, small green squash, called *zapallitos de tronco*, are eaten filled with a mix of onions, meat, or rice. Also in Argentina, a stew made of squash, rice, meat, and other foods, called *carbonada de zapallo,* is served inside a *zapallo* squash.

En México, las calabacitas pequeñas se cocinan con crema y chiles. En Argentina, unas calabacitas verdes, llamadas zapallitos de tronco se comen rellenas de cebolla, carne o arroz. También en Argentina, la carbonada, un guisado de arroz, maíz, carne y otros ingredientes, se sirve dentro de una calabaza o zapallo horneado.

Squash blossoms, or flowers, are another Latin American treat. Sometimes squash blossoms are covered in a batter and fried. They also make a great filling for quesadillas. Squash blossoms also add beautiful color and a nice **crunch** to soups and salads.

Las flores de la calabaza son otro convite latinoamericano. En ocasiones, las flores de calabaza se **rebozan** y fríen. También son muy ricas en quesadillas. Las flores de calabaza, además, le dan mucho color y textura a las sopas y ensaladas.

19

Within the last 500 years, squash has spread around the world. New kinds of squash have **evolved**. Zucchini, which is now eaten across Latin America, was first grown in Europe. People have found new ways of cooking squash, too. In Korea, pumpkins are often served boiled.

En los últimos 500 años las calabazas se han difundido por todo el mundo. Nuevos tipos de calabazas han **evolucionado**. El calabacín, que hoy se come mucho en Latinoamérica, se cultivó primero en Europa. En Corea, a menudo, las calabazas se comen hervidas.

People around the world have found new ways to use squash, too. In the United States and Canada, people cut funny or scary faces in big, orange pumpkins on Halloween. Squash is one outstanding crop. There are so many ways to enjoy it!

En todo el mundo la gente disfruta de las calabazas. En los Estados Unidos y Canadá se acostumbra cortar caras curiosas y de miedo en las calabazas durante Halloween. Las calabazas son un extraordinario cultivo. ¡Hay muchas maneras de disfrutar de su rico sabor!

GLOSSARY

crunch (KRUNCH) A loud chewing sound.

evolved (ih-VOLVD) Changed over time.

lobed (LOHBD) Having a curved or rounded part that sticks out or down.

mashed (MASH-ed) Made into a soft mass.

pollinate (PAH-luh-nayt) To move pollen around to different plants, which helps them make seeds.

scientists (SY-un-tists) People who study the world.

vines (VYNZ) The long, winding stems of plants.

GLOSARIO

científicos (los) Personas que estudian el mundo.

evolucionar Cambiar con el tiempo.

lóbulos (los) Partes redondeadas que sobresalen de una fruta o verdura.

polinizar Mover el polen de una parte a otra de una planta para ayudarles a crear semillas.

puré (el) Comida que se prepara triturando legumbres o verduras cocidas.

rebozar Cubrir con harina y huevo un alimento antes de freírlo.

trepadoras (las) Plantas que crecen y se sostienen en un armazón.

INDEX

B
bees, 9

C
crop, 5, 22
crunch, 18

G
güicoys, 6

K
kinds, 5–6, 10, 21

N
North America, 5

P
pumpkins, 6, 14, 21–22

S
scientists, 9–10

South America, 5

V
vines, 9

ÍNDICE

A
abejas, 9
continente americano, 5

C
científicos, 9–10
cultivo, 5, 22

G
guicoyas, 6

T
tipos, 5–6, 10, 21
trepadoras, 9

WEB SITES / PÁGINAS DE INTERNET

Due to the changing nature of Internet links, PowerKids Press and Editorial Buenas Letras have developed an online list of Web sites related to the subject of this book. This site is updated regularly. Please use this link to access the list: www.powerkidslinks.com/nfla/squash/